AVON SUPERSTARS

T5-DHF-034

DOUG FLUTIE

Barbara Siegel & Scott Siegel

AVON SUPERSTARS

For Daniel & Evan

AVON BOOKS
A division of
The Hearst Corporation
1790 Broadway
New York, New York 10019

Copyright © 1985 by Avon Books
Published by arrangement with Parachute Press
ISBN: 0-380-75040-6

First Avon Printing, August 1985

AVON TRADEMARK REG. U. S. PAT. OFF. AND IN
OTHER COUNTRIES. MARCA REGISTRADA. HECHO EN
U. S. A.

Printed in the U. S. A.

OP   10   9   8   7   6   5   4   3   2   1

1

"The Pass"
November 23, 1984

The clock was stopped with just six seconds left in what was about to become one of the most famous college football games of all time. Doug Flutie's Boston College team was losing to the University of Miami by a score of 45-41. Flutie and his Eagles had the ball on the Miami 48-yard line. This was going to be the last play of the game—a play that no one who saw the game will ever forget. . . .

From the opening kickoff, it had been a battle. The two premier quarterbacks in college football had finally come face-to-face in a classic match-up. Bernie Kosar of the University of Miami was everything that Doug Flutie was not. He was tall and strong—a classic drop-back, pocket passer.

On the other hand, at 5 feet 9 inches and 176 pounds, Doug Flutie seemed way too short to compete effectively against the likes of Kosar and his mighty Miami team, the defending college champions. And Flutie was anything but a classic drop-back, pocket passer. He was a scrambler. He seemed to score as many points by doing things from broken plays as he did doing them from designed ones.

Flutie had led the surprising Boston College Eagles to a record of 7 wins and 2 losses, a national ranking in the top 10, and a guarantee that they'd play in the Cotton Bowl at the end of the year. He was already college football's all-time leader in total yardage, and every yard he gained now added to that record. He was being touted as a possible Heisman Trophy winner as the top college player of 1984. He'd done all of that, and yet, because of his size, there were still a lot of people who didn't think he could really play big-time football.

In this game, in front of a national TV audience, against Bernie Kosar, the other top-rated college quarterback, Flutie had his chance to give the doubters something to think about—and to finally silence them.

It was not a great day for a football game. There was a blustery wind and a steady rain. But the game started really well for Doug. He completed his first 11 passes. In front of the stunned hometown Miami fans, Boston jumped out to a 14-0 lead!

Then Bernie Kosar got hot. In one stretch, he went 11 for 11 just as Doug had done—and he brought Miami roaring back to a 14-14 tie.

From that point on, the game seesawed back

and forth. Neither team took a commanding lead. Both kept right on scoring, matching each other's drives up and down the field. At the half, Boston led 28-21, but the way these two offensive powerhouses kept putting points up on the board, it seemed as if the scoreboard would run out of numbers before the game was over.

In the second half the two teams came at each other like locomotives. Neither Boston nor Miami would give in to the pressure. They just kept hammering at each other, with Kosar firing his passes out of the pocket and Flutie scrambling and throwing on the run, turning broken plays into big gainers.

Late in the fourth quarter, with less than three minutes left in the game, Boston was leading by a score of 41-38.

It looked as if Boston's defense was finally holding. They had Bernie Kosar and the Miami Hurricanes at third down and 21 yards to go, deep in Miami territory. It seemed hopeless. But then Kosar threw a pass that was good for 20 yards. On fourth and one, it was their last play if they didn't make it. They had to make it. They did. Miami gained five. The Hurricanes now began to move steadily down the field, eating up the yards as well as the time on the clock. Time was ticking down . . .

Kosar did everything that was expected of him. He was the classic quarterback leading his team to victory. With less than a minute left, Miami scored the go-ahead touchdown when Bernie handed off to his fullback, who plunged one yard into the Boston end zone. It was 45-41, and Miami's offense ran off the field screaming and yelling that they had won it! The Miami fans went wild! They were jumping up and down yelling, "We're number one! We're number one!"

It looked like the end for B.C. But as far as Doug Flutie was concerned, the game wasn't over yet.

After the kickoff, Flutie took over on his own 20-yard line with just 28 seconds left in the game. When he was asked later what was on his mind when he ran onto the field, Flutie said, "All I was thinking was, 'They [his teammates] played well, they deserve it. All we have to do is get the ball to midfield. Then we're in range to just throw it into the end zone.' "

When Flutie went into the huddle, he let his teammates know he hadn't given up. He told them, "We can do it!"

He'd done it for them all year long. He'd done it for them ever since he became the starting quarterback in his freshman year four years ago. And if they believed in anyone, they believed in Doug Flutie.

He said they could do it. Well, then, maybe they could. They broke out of their huddle with confidence. On the sideline, Bernie Kosar and the rest of the Miami offense were celebrating. They thought they had the game all wrapped up.

Flutie took the snap and threw a 19-yard pass.

Into the air went a referee's flag. Penalty. Miami was caught holding. Boston College was a little farther down the field, but they still had a very long way to go. And now there were just 20 seconds left on the clock.

On the next play, Flutie scrambled out of the pocket, ran toward the line of scrimmage, and then, at the last second, threw to Scott Gieselman, who caught the ball and ran it out of bounds on the Miami 48-yard line.

Flutie wanted to be at midfield—and now he was there! Miami had stopped celebrating.

He figured he had time for two more plays. Rather than go for the end zone at this point and risk an interception, he decided to throw a pass to the Miami 25-yard line to set up an easier pass on the next play. The play that would be the last one in the game.

The pass fell incomplete.

And now there were just six seconds left. . . .

The Boston coach, Jack Bicknell, sent in a player from the bench with instructions, but Flutie waved him back to the sideline. He knew what the play was going to be. They called it

"55 Flood Tip." The play called for sending every available receiver into the end zone. When they got near the goal line, it was Flutie's job to heave the ball in their general direction. As Doug put it, "You throw and pray . . . it's a 50-50 chance your guy will come up with it."

Up to this point, Doug had thrown 45 passes and completed 33. He'd thrown two touchdown passes and not a single interception. He'd shown he had the heart of a lion, the skills of a great quarterback, and the leadership of a great field general. And now he wanted to show everyone that he was a winner.

Boston College broke from the huddle and lined up. Flutie looked over the defense. Miami knew what was coming. Everybody knew what was coming. The people in the stands and the national TV audience knew that Flutie was throwing for the goal line. Only Doug, it seemed, thought he had a 50-50 chance. The millions of people watching Boston College and Miami fight it out knew that it would take a miracle for Flutie to win this game.

He took the snap. Four Boston College receivers raced toward the Miami end zone. Meanwhile, though, Flutie was under pressure from the Miami pass rush. He'd been dodging them all day long and he'd have do it one more time. He ran out of the grasp of left tackle Jerome Brown and ran to his right, trying to give his receivers a chance to get farther downfield.

Flutie was at his own 38-yard line when he set himself and threw a bullet that seemed surprisingly low for a pass that needed to fly at least 62 yards.

There was one second left on the clock when he let it go. There would be no second chance.

Miami safety Darrell Fullington saw Flutie's pass coming. He was covering Gerard Phelan, Flutie's roommate and favorite receiver. Fullington couldn't believe that Flutie could throw the ball that far. There just was no way that a little guy like that could throw a low pass two thirds the length of the football field. He let Phelan get behind him and ran up five yards to make what he thought would be the game-ending interception.

But the ball just wouldn't come down!

It sailed over Fullington's outstretched hands and hit Gerard Phelan right in the chest. He wrapped his arms around it as he fell down in the end zone. Then he jumped up and showed the ref he'd caught it!

TOUCHDOWN!

The fans in the stadium went wild, and millions of people watching on TV were stunned. It was such an unbelievable play! And it was amusing, too, that the person who caused all the excitement was the last one to know what had happened.

Doug's view was partially blocked by all the big lineman. "I thought the pass was incomplete," he said afterwards. "I saw the ref's arms go up, but I didn't believe him. Then I looked over on the Miami sideline and they were all just standing there."

That's when he knew.

The final score was Boston College 47, Miami 45.

And "The Pass" was history.

In the locker room after the game, Boston's Mark MacDonald said, "That wasn't Gerard Phelan who caught that ball . . . God caught that ball."

But Jim Ostrowski, a Boston lineman, disagreed. "No," he said, "God threw it."

2
Growing Up

"The Pass" made Doug Flutie a national hero. But it didn't go to his head. Doug was used to cheering crowds because he had *always* been a star performer. Whether it was in college, high school, Little League—even Midget League—he somehow managed to get everyone rooting for him. And why not? He always found the most exciting ways to won.

Probably the biggest win of his life, though, was being born to Dick and Joan Flutie on October 23, 1962. His next biggest victory was having two brothers who loved sports almost as much as he did.

Growing up in Melbourne, Florida, Doug and his two brothers, Bill (the oldest) and Darren (the youngest), spent practically all their time out in the sunshine playing one sport or another. It hardly seemed to matter what they did as long as they were competing at something.

According to Bill, "Doug always had to be playing. He used to make up games, and they were serious games. Hall football. Cup baseball. Crush a snow-cone cup, hit it with your hand, and go around the bases." Well, at least they were serious to Doug.

When all three boys (who are fairly close in age) showed so much interest in sports, their father, Dick Flutie, made a decision. His now-famous son put it best: "My dad had very little interest in athletics, but once we got into it, he wanted to be a part of it. He coached us all our lives when we were young. He wanted to get into the swing of things because he knew it was important to us—we enjoyed it, we excelled at it—he wanted to be a part of it with us, and that was important to him . . . *and to us.*"

Dick and Joan Flutie weren't rich people. But Mr. Flutie decided to get personally involved in helping his sons reach their full sports potential. Money wasn't the issue. He sent his boys off to sports camps every summer, even though it was expensive. He did it because he wanted to. And to this day, and probably for the rest of his life, Doug Flutie will be thankful for his father's caring. Doug said, "He was excellent in helping us. Whenever we needed something athletically, he was always there. He wanted to be a part of whatever *we* were a part of. And that really helped us all along and got us going."

Doug said that most kids who ultimately succeed in sports have a close relationship with their parents. "I think that's the key when you're growing up," he said, "because your parents have to *back* you. They have to be there to drive you to the Little League field every week."

Doug's parents not only drove their sons to the field, they stayed to cheer them on.

They were there when Doug played shortstop in an all-star game, and saw him scoop up a hot grounder, pretend to make a throw to first base, and then make a tremendous leap to reach the runner going past him from second to third and tag him out. And at the end of the game they were there to see him named Most Valuable Player.

Although all three Flutie boys were active in sports, it was Doug who seemed to have that special flare. Even his mother later admitted to a Boston sportswriter, "Watching Doug was always a thrill. Bill, our oldest son, always did well. He got the play done. But even if Doug wasn't doing something exactly right, it would still be more fun to watch him play. Even if the others were better."

With three first-rate athletes around, there was a lot of competition in the Flutie household. Each one of them wanted to be the best. Their father taught them to win, and they would really go at it with each other. Doug laughs at the memory of how hard they tried to win when they played one another. "Yeah, you get in arguments and fights . . . you get in situations where you're out on the driveway and playing one-on-one . . . and that's competitive!"

Luckily, though, organized sports came along and saved them from beating one another's brains out. Doug explained, "By the age of ten or twelve, we were working together. We were on the same teams, and [instead of competing against each other] it was always to beat a common opponent." Doug smiles when he thinks about those moments when the Flutie family pulled off one of their dazzling plays. "We'd really go after them. And it was great because there was a lot of teamwork between us . . . we helped each other."

Doug's closest childhood friendships were with the boys who shared his interest in sports. "I had friends at school, but my closest friends were the athletes that I played with," Doug said. "On the Little League field or basketball court, we were all in the same circle. Our interests rubbed off on each other and we became friends."

Whatever friends he had made in Melbourne, though, he would soon have to leave behind.

The Flutie family was moving on. From the sunshine of Florida, they moved up to cold New England. They made their new home in Natick, Massachusetts.

It was 1976.

Doug was the new kid in a new junior high school, but he was the same old Doug. He played as hard as he could. And it wasn't very long before Tom Lamb, the Natick High School football coach, started hearing about this great young player he'd soon be seeing.

3
Choosing Football

In 1978, Doug was a sophomore and on the Natick High football team. But he wasn't the quarterback. His older brother, Bill, held that position.

Unlike most high school sophomores, Doug had already just about reached his full height. He was five feet eight inches tall. He'd grow one more inch by the time he was a pro. As for his weight, he was much scrawnier than he is now. He was officially 150 pounds during that first season of playing high school varsity football. By the time he played for the New Jersey Generals seven years later, he would put on another 26 pounds—all of it muscle.

Before the 1978 season started, Doug was just a second-string defensive back. During practice, however, he showed what he could do and was given a shot at the first-string assignment.

Doug didn't waste any time turning his defensive job into an offensive one. In his very first game—the season opener for Natick High—he decided to blitz. He found an opening in the offensive line and roared into the enemy backfield. The ball was handed off to the full-back—a fullback who outweighed Doug by more than 50 pounds. Doug didn't hesitate. He went after the ball carrier. Coach Tom Lamb tells the rest: "Somehow Doug came out of the pile with the ball. He ran all the way to the 15-yard line. We scored and won the game 6-0."

That was just a small indication of what was to come. Later that year, Doug won the starting quarterback job from his brother. But as Doug said, they had learned how to help each other. And Bill soon became his kid brother's favorite receiver. Two Fluties can't play 11 positions though, and the team, according to coach Tom Lamb, wasn't very good. "We spent the first half following the game plan," said the coach to a reporter. "But eventually, we would go into the shotgun formation and let Doug throw every time."

Doug's favorite high school game was during his sophomore year. It was the last game of the season, and Natick High was losing to Braintree High by a score of 25-24.

Time was running out.

In classic Doug Flutie style, he rallied his team and led them down the field. And how did he do it? He threw four completions in a row to his brother Bill. But they got only as far as the Braintree 21-yard line with just three seconds left on the scoreboard clock.

Natick High called for a time-out.

They needed a 38-yard field goal to win the game. There aren't many high school kickers who could lift one through the crossbars at that distance. But Doug told his coach that he wanted to try kicking for the field goal. This was quite a surprise. He had never tried a field goal in any game during the season. But he believed he could do it, and he convinced the coach. He got the green light.

With his brother Bill taking the snap and holding the ball, Doug stepped into it and gave it everything he had. The ball lifted up over the outstretched hands of the Braintree defenders and soared up into the air toward the goalpost. It was straight and true . . . but was it long enough?

When Doug's mother heard the crowd erupt in cheers and wild applause, she knew Doug had done it. But she hadn't seen it. She had gotten so nervous that she left the stands.

His ability as a placekicker isn't well known, but when asked if he could do the job today if he was pressed into service for the Generals, he said proudly: "I could kick up to 40 yards." And then he laughed and added that he doubted he'd ever be needed. Don't be surprised, though, if someday you see him win a pro game with an extra point or a field goal. He'll do anything he can to help his team win.

It was during his first year in high school that Doug met the girl he would later marry. In fact, he met her on the very first day of class. All the students were assigned their homeroom classes based on alphabetical order. Therefore, all the "Fs" were in one class. And that put Doug Flutie and Laurie Fortier right next to each other. According to *People* magazine, Doug didn't waste any time finding out who this pretty, dark-haired girl was. He snuck a peek at her notebook to find out her name and then made sure to be at the right place at the right time so he could get acquainted.

Doug's love of sports even entered into his social life. He took Laurie to a Boston Red Sox baseball game on his first date with her. They managed to spend even more time together (or at least near each other) when Doug was playing. How? Because Laurie became a cheerleader!

Near the end of their sophomore year together, on June 12th, Doug asked her to go steady with him. She said yes. At Christmas, 1984, just before he signed his contract with the New Jersey Generals, he asked Laurie to marry him. And she said yes again. In the summer of 1985, Doug and Laurie got married. This time she didn't say yes, she said, "I do."

While he was dating Laurie, Doug was also

busy making quite a name for himself in high school sports. Doug not only proved himself a great football player, he showed that he was an extremely gifted all-around athlete. By the time he was a senior, he had earned an amazing eight varsity letters! You receive a "letter" (your school's initial) for each year you play a varsity sport.

On the Natick High baseball team, he played shortstop when he wasn't pitching. With his great speed and quick reflexes, he was the kind of shortstop who could go deep into the hole for a hard grounder and still make the play. And as for his pitching, the well-known power of Doug's throwing arm makes it easy to imagine him blazing fastballs past opposing batters.

On the Natick High basketball team, Doug played point guard. And he played it remarkably well. Well enough, in fact, to be considered the best in all of Massachusetts and be named as a Bay State All-Star.

During his high school football career, Doug made the prestigious *Boston Globe* all-star team twice. This was a big honor. It meant he was one of the state's top players. The first time he was named an all-star was during his sophomore year, and he made it as a defensive back. His second all-star selection was, of course, as a quarterback.

He was so good at all three major sports—baseball, basketball, and football—that he might have had a chance to make it in any one. And surprisingly, football was not his favorite! He said, "I was excited about my basketball chances. That was a thrill to me: basketball. When it came to picking, I didn't really want to choose, but it was sort of dictated to me that football was the one."

The decision was made for him because nobody was offering him college scholarships in basketball or baseball. But there was some interest in him as a football player. Doug said, "Football scholarships were there, and that's what pointed me in that direction."

Though there were schools interested in recruiting Doug for their college football programs, they weren't exactly beating down his door. Despite a solid A average and his impressive athletic achievements, he was usually considered too small by most coaches to be effective in big-time college football.

This issue of his size—he was now at his full height of 5'9"—was to plague him throughout his career. But when he first heard that the head coach of Boston College had decided not to recruit him because of his size, Doug couldn't believe it. "Height?" he said with disbelief. "I never even thought about height."

Luckily for Doug—and for Boston College—

there was a change in head coaches. Until then, he had been considering Brown, where his brother Bill was going to school and playing football. He was also thinking about Harvard (which, like Brown, didn't offer any athletic scholarships), the University of New Hampshire, and Holy Cross. But Boston College was where he really wanted to play. And when the new head coach, Jack Bicknell, offered him a scholarship and a shot at the quarterback position, Doug grabbed it.

It was off to Boston College—and into the record books.

4
Fourth-String Quarterback

Jack Bicknell promised Doug a chance at winning the quarterback job, but when he arrived at his first practice that August, Doug found he was listed as a receiver. He later told a reporter, "I had convinced myself that I wasn't going to be a quarterback. I thought I'd be a defensive back or receiver." And then he added, "It didn't matter as long as I could play major college football."

The Boston College coaches didn't know what to do with Doug. Though he was listed as a wide receiver, they let him practice with the other quarterbacks, but they also thought he might make it as a first-string safety. So how did they use him for their first game of the season against Texas A & M? He was sent in as a punt returner!

The Boston College Eagles squeaked out a 13-12 victory in that opening game, but it was downhill from there. Their next game was against ninth-ranked North Carolina. Boston was slaughtered 56-14. But there wasn't much for the freshman to do but look on helplessly. The coaches still hadn't figured out what they should do with him.

In their third game of the season, Boston College played West Virginia. And the story was the same: trounced! The final score was 38-10.

One of Boston's problems in their first three games was at quarterback. Between injuries and too many incomplete passes, the offense just wasn't getting the job done. Their next opponent was mighty Penn State, which was always a power in the East, and Coach Bicknell was worried. "I just hope we have a healthy quarterback situation for Penn State," he told a reporter, "because we have to throw the ball down there. That's for sure."

The first half was a nightmare. Penn State seemed to score every time they had the ball. Boston College could barely get a first down. In their last two games, the Eagles might have lost, but at least they put some points on the board. But a team can't score when it doesn't move the ball. When the gun sounded ending the second quarter, Penn State was on top 24-0.

While the bands played during the halftime break, the Boston College coaches talked things over in the locker room. They weren't getting anywhere with their first-, second-, or third-string quarterbacks. They decided that if the third quarter went like the first two, they'd give the freshman quarterback the ball. They figured they had nothing to lose.

The receivers' coach, Barry Gallup, went over to Doug and said, "You'd better be ready. I think you're going to get a shot."

During the third quarter, Penn State scored two more touchdowns and led 38-0. Boston was playing like zombies. Meanwhile, Doug was warming up on the sideline. Coach Gallup remembers watching Doug and he said later, "You could see he was getting more and more excited. He wasn't thinking about the 85,000 screaming Penn State fans. He was just having fun."

Then, as the fourth quarter was about to start, the Eagles' head coach Jack Bicknell said, "Okay, Flutie. See what you can do."

It must have seemed like pure desperation to send in a freshman against Penn State in front of all those screaming fans. And it was.

Boston College had the ball at their own 22-yard line, 78 *long* yards away from the Penn State goal. It had been the same story all day long—the offense buried deep in their own territory. Doug had to do something to spark the team. Boston had managed just *two yards* in total passing yardage in the first three quarters. That was the first thing he was going to change. On third down, he threw his first collegiate pass—and his first completion! It was for 15 yards and a first down.

The team seemed to come to life under his

leadership. He masterminded another first down when he faked out the defense with a draw play to one of his running backs. Now both Flutie and the rest of the offense were gaining confidence. They were moving down the field. Doug threw the ball—and hit his receiver for a 20-yard gain that put the Eagles on the Penn State 23-yard line.

Winning the game was out of the question—Penn led by 38. It was now a matter of pride. Scoring a touchdown to avoid the shutout would sure help. And that's what Doug went after when he threw his third pass of his college career toward the left corner of the Penn State end zone. The receiver he was trying to hit was his tight end, Scott Nizolek. And Nizolek grabbed it for the TD!

Even Flutie was surprised that they had actually marched the length of the field and scored. "It was like, 'I don't believe it,' " he admitted.

And then he nearly did it again!

With time running out, he once more led the Eagles toward the Penn State goal line. He almost scored. But on a fourth-down play he was intercepted on the Penn State 2-yard line. Just the same, he had made quite an impression. In just one quarter of play, he had racked up 135 yards in the air. But more than that, he had fired up the whole team. Even the defense came to life, stopping Penn State from scoring in the fourth quarter.

"It was like somebody hit a switch and the tempo picked up," recalled Coach Bicknell. "Never, ever could we imagine what we had." He was referring, of course, to Doug Flutie.

5
Breakthrough!

As far as Coach Bicknell was concerned, Doug had earned a chance to be the starting quarterback the following week against Navy. In that game, he threw for 118 yards and went 14 for 25, but it wasn't enough. Navy was too strong and beat B.C. 25-10. Doug seemed to be feeling his way along. It was only his first full game at quarterback and he was probably a little bit nervous.

Their next game was against Army, and Bicknell decided to go with Doug one more time. He wasn't sorry. His new quarterback seemed to suddenly catch fire. Not only did he also complete 15 out of 21 passes for 244 yards, he threw for three touchdowns. Boston destroyed Army 41-6.

Doug was starting to turn the team around. But their next opponent was Pittsburgh—with Dan Marino at quarterback. The Panthers were ranked #2 in the nation with the number-one defense. What could a freshman quarterback with slightly better than two games worth of experience do against a team like that?

It looked like a mismatch—especially when

Pitt started to pull away in the third quarter with a 29-10 lead. But Doug brought B.C. roaring back with an 88-yard drive that he capped with a 30-yard touchdown pass.

In the cheering hometown crowd were Doug's parents. Joan Flutie turned to her husband and said, "I can't believe it! He looks like he's out there playing with his brothers. I've been watching this all my life."

The next time B.C. got the ball, Flutie threw another touchdown pass! All of a sudden, it was 29-24, and the Eagles were within striking distance. But they never got into the end zone again. Neither team scored and Pitt won by five points. But both Flutie and his teammates had learned they could play with the best and hold their own. So even though they lost, their confidence began to soar.

Jack Bicknell talked about his quarterback after that game. "You look at him, look at his poise for being so young, look at the things he does and just hope we don't ruin him. He believes in everything he does. He's flipping the ball around, doing some really goofy things— and they work. You watch him and just hope you don't coach all that out of him."

Bicknell was starting to realize just how special Doug Flutie was.

The following week, a Flutie-led Boston College team beat the University of Massachusetts 52-22. Then they lost a heartbreaker to Syracuse, 27-17. They bounced back with a tough win over Rutgers, 27-21, despite a relatively poor performance by Doug. And then, in the final game of the season against Holy Cross, the Flutie magic was there again and he led his team to a dramatic 28-24 victory.

For the season, Boston finished with a record of five wins and six losses. But in the seven games that Doug Flutie started that year, Boston won four and lost three.

Next season looked *very* promising.

Like the year before, B.C.'s season opener was against Texas A & M. The pre-season polls had the Aggies from Texas in the top 20. Boston wasn't ranked anywhere by anyone. Though Boston had beaten Texas A & M last year, Boston was picked to lose by 15 points! Playing in Texas, under a broiling sun, the team from New England put on quite a show. And the star performer was Doug Flutie.

Doug threw 26 passes and completed 18. His total yardage through the air was a whopping 356 yards. His three touchdown passes helped Boston to a decisive 38-16 triumph.

This Boston College team was for real. And so was their quarterback. But looming ahead, after such a wonderful start, was a match-up they weren't sure they were ready for. Doug was going to have to lead them against the #1 ranked team in the country: Clemson.

In some sections of the country, the Boston–Clemson game was being shown on TV. For the first time, Doug would get to show what he could do in front of millions of people. He didn't want to let the viewers—or his team—down.

Boston College was a 12-point underdog. A lot of people thought it should have been more like 18 points. At the half, it looked as if they were right. Boston was losing 14-0. But the second half was like an entirely different game. First, Doug led the Eagles on a 72-yard drive into the Clemson end zone for a touchdown. Then he drove down the field again for another 61 yards, capped off with a 36-yard TD pass.

The two teams traded field goals and they were tied at 17 each. And that was how the game ended. In the record books, it was a tie. But when an unranked, unknown team plays against the #1 ranked college team in the nation and can walk away without a loss, that's a very special sort of victory that can't be described in a record book.

There was something else that came out of that game that you'd never see in a record book. It was the birth of a star. Everybody loves an underdog, and a lot of those people watching the game on TV fell in love with Doug Flutie.

Newspapers and TV stations started following Doug, writing articles and profiles about him. He was fast becoming much more than just a local hero.

Doug and his teammates were winning the respect of fans all across the country. And they were also winning football games. They sunk Navy 31-0, with Doug throwing three touchdown passes. They beat Temple, but lost to West Virginia—both were close games. Then they rebounded with a win over Rutgers. And they kept on winning, rolling over Army. But then they came up against Penn State again, the team that Doug first played against in the final quarter the year before. He had passed for one touchdown in that game, which the Eagles lost 38-7. In this game, he managed to get 17 points up on the board. But it wasn't anywhere near what they needed. Penn State slaughtered Boston College 52-17. It was enough to dishearten any team, but this year, because of their strong showing, Boston had a chance to win a berth in a bowl game. They had to play well during the rest of the season; they couldn't afford to let down. They had two games left, and Doug rallied them to victories in both. They beat the University of Massachusetts 34-21 and Holy Cross 35-10.

They made it to the Tangerine Bowl!

They were set to play a tough Auburn team.

Doug Flutie, Quarterback
New Jersey Generals

Doug prepares to throw "The Pass ."

"The Pass" saved the game, but scrambling like this saves Doug!
UPI/Bettmann Newsphotos

Doug breaks the NCAA record for total offense—9,723 yards!

Doug signs an autograph for a faithful fan.
A/P Wide World Photos

Doug accepts the Cotton Bowl trophy on behalf of his Boston College team.
A/P Wide World Photos

Now that's team work! Doug's BC teammates help him celebrate his 22nd birthday!
A/P Wide World Photos

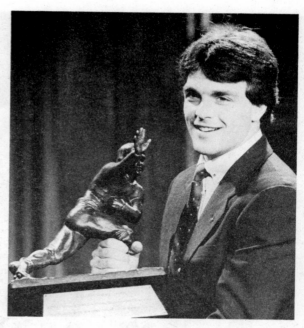

Doug accepts
the Heisman
Trophy . . .
UPI/Bettmann
Newsphotos

. . . and the
congratulations
of his family and
fiance, Laurie.
A/P Wide World Photos

Being a top college athlete isn't all hard work. Doug clowns around with Mary Lou Retton on a Bob Hope TV special.
AP/Wide World Photos

Meet General Flutie! Doug shows off his new shirt to Generals' owner,
Donald Trump.
UPI/Bettmann Newsphotos

Doug looks downfield for a receiver . . .
New Jersey Generals

Doug prepares a pass . . .
New Jersey Generals

The perfect Flutie form . . .
New Jersey Generals

But sometimes you get company. Doug under pressure!
UPI/Bettmann Newsphotos

The Dynamite Duo—Doug Flutie and Herschel Walker.
A/P Wide World Photos

Doug Flutie . . . he's only just begun . . .
New Jersey Generals

Everybody knew that they'd have to play their best to win. Being in a bowl game and knowing that the game was being seen on TV all across the country seemed to make Doug and his teammates freeze up. Boston was trailing 23-10 at the half and Doug later said, "I hate to admit it, but I was tight the first half." That was obvious from his statistics: Doug had completed only 10 out of 22 passes and two thrown interceptions. But the Eagles came back in the second half and outplayed Auburn—only to fall short by a single touchdown. They lost the game 33-26.

Including the loss in the Tangerine Bowl, they had finished the 1982 season with a 8-3-1 record and almost made it into the top 20, coming in 25th in the nation. And they did it with a sophomore quarterback who was still learning. It had been a great year for Doug and Boston College, but they knew they could do even better. Even as the season ended, they were looking forward to 1983.

6
They Can't Stop Flutie!

What does a star quarterback do between football seasons? For one, he switched from studying computer science to communications. He figured that with all the interviews he was giving, he was already getting a pretty good education in journalism.

And when summer came, the athlete who helped pack the stadium with adoring fans was doing a different sort of packing—packing a synthetic sod on the football field for seven dollars an hour.

He could barely wait for the season to start.

The 1983 opener was against Morgan State. By now, opposing teams knew that the best way to stop Boston College was to stop Doug Flutie. Morgan State didn't do a very good job of it. Doug threw for 227 yards and three touchdowns. And in this, his first game as a junior, he broke the Boston College career passing mark of 4,555 yards.

But then Morgan State almost broke *him!* After a sack, he was pinned at the bottom of the pile. Doug felt his ankle being twisted and thought a Morgan State player was doing it deliberately. "I kicked him, trying to get away," Doug later told reporters. "When I kicked at him, he retaliated." And that caused a near brawl on the field, as Boston's players jumped in to protect their quarterback. As one Eagles' player put it, "We don't like people jumping on Flutie."

It was a good thing they felt that way, because their next game was against Clemson. There wasn't any secret about what the Clemson players were thinking: They wanted revenge for the way Boston College embarrassed them the year before and knocked them from their #1 ranking. And just like Morgan State, they were basing their strategy on stopping Doug Flutie. In fact, they were telling the press that they were planning a "ten-man rush of Flutie."

It seemed to work. At the end of the first half, Clemson had shut down the Boston College offense and led 13-3. In the second half, though, B.C. fought back. If Clemson wouldn't give them the pass, then they'd run the ball. And once the running game started working, Doug was free to throw again. Keeping the Clemson defense off balance, the Eagles started putting touchdown after touchdown up on the scoreboard. Clemson was shocked by the onslaught. When the gun sounded at the end of the game, the final score was Boston College 31, Clemson 16.

The Eagles were a team of destiny—and their quarterback was their ticket to greatness.

Except for a loss against West Virginia, Flutie and the Eagles steamrolled over their competition week after week. They murdered Rutgers 42-22, even though Doug was knocked out of the game with a concussion. They got by a pesky Temple team 18-15, and buried Yale 42-7, with Doug throwing four touchdown passes.

Boston College had finally broken into the top 20 ranking at #19. But now they had to play Penn State—a team the Eagles had *never* beaten in their entire history. On top of that, Penn State had already beaten highly-rated West Virginia (who had defeated Boston College earlier in the season) and Alabama. It seemed very likely that the Eagles would have a very short stay in the top 20. At least that's what the Penn State players were probably thinking.

Doug Flutie seemed to thrive on the heroic, impossible comeback, but in this game he led his team to a quick 21-0 lead, and then they hung on. He gained an incredible 380 yards through the air (with two touchdown passes) and dazed the Penn State defense as he was dazzling a national TV audience. The final score was Boston College 27, Penn State 17.

Even Doug Flutie seemed stunned with what they had done. With both pride and a touch of surprise in his voice, he said, "Penn State . . . we're on a level with Penn State!"

In fact—at that magic moment—they were on a *higher* level than Penn State. And they were still rising in the polls!

In their next game, Doug threw for 262 yards and four touchdowns and bombed Army 34-14. But every game can't be a winner. Doug had a terrible day when they played Syracuse, throwing 36 passes but completing only 12. Worse than that, though, he threw three interceptions. Boston College lost 21-10. Coach Bicknell felt sorrier for Doug than he did for himself. "I have to keep telling people," he said, "that the kid is just a kid."

But the "kid" didn't have two bad games in a row. He led Boston to a 47-7 rout of Holy Cross and then stunned #13 Alabama with a 20-13 victory in front of another national TV audience.

Boston College finished its regular season with an 8-2 record and was ranked #13 in the nation. On the strength of that record, they were invited to the Liberty Bowl to play Notre Dame. And in one of the most exciting bowl games of the year, Boston College lost by a single point, 19-18. Doug threw for nearly 300 yards and passed for three TDs—but it wasn't enough to win. It was enough, however, to have Doug named the game's Most Valuable Player.

It's almost unheard of to award an MVP to a member of the losing team, but Doug's tremendous performance couldn't be denied.

Doug had brought the Eagles to two bowl games so far, but had yet to win. They all believed they were good enough to get into a major bowl game again next year. This time, though, they were going to win it! And why not? Doug was going into his senior year and he was getting better all the time!

7
The Heisman Trophy

At the end of the 1983 football season, Doug had been startled to discover that he was being seriously considered for the Heisman Trophy, the award given to the outstanding college football player of the year. It had come down to three finalists: Nebraska's Mike Rozier, Brigham Young's Steve Young—and Boston College's Doug Flutie!

Not for one minute, though, did Doug think he was going to win. It had been more than a decade since they had given the award to a quarterback, and that was the position that both he and Steve Young played. But what really convinced him that he wouldn't win was the fact that he was a junior, while the other two were seniors.

Doug was right. Mike Rozier, a running back, won the Heisman Trophy.

But now Doug was considered a leading contender for the 1984 Heisman. Playing well wouldn't be enough. He had to play great . . . and win!

At the beginning of the 1984 college football season, Doug was getting a lot of media attention. Not only was he a leading contender for the Heisman Trophy, and playing on one of the top-ranked teams in the East, he also had that special quality called charisma.

The camera loved his good-looking, boyish face. Journalists loved him because he was smart and gave intelligent, thoughtful answers to their questions. And the fans loved him because he was the most exciting college player to have come along in more than a decade. He was electrifying to watch on the field because you never knew what he was going to do.

The media also played up his "good-guy" image. He was the kind of guy you'd be proud to call your friend. He was an old-fashioned young man who didn't smoke or drink. He had a great relationship with his family, and he didn't ditch his girl friend when he became famous. His best friend and roommate was Gerard Phelan, who was also his favorite pass receiver.

And now there was a new dimension: He'd be playing with his kid brother, Darren, who had just been recruited to play for Boston College. It was getting to be a family show.

Everyone who followed college football in 1984 was keeping his eyes on Doug. All those people across the country who had become his fans were hoping that this year would be the crowning glory of his four years at Boston College.

The first game of the new season was against highly rated Western Carolina. Doug threw for 330 yards and four touchdowns. The final score had Boston on top, 44-24. It had been an easy win, but the next game was going to be much tougher. It was against Alabama *in* Alabama. Boston had beaten them last year, but who ever beat mighty Alabama twice in a row? It sure didn't look as if it was going to be Boston College when they fell behind 31-14 at the beginning of the third quarter. But the Eagles' defense stopped Alabama from scoring again and Doug led them on drive after drive into the Crimson Tide's end zone. He threw for 254 yards and two touchdowns—and when the game ended, the scoreboard read: Boston College 38, Alabama 31.

This game was shown on national TV during prime time. More people saw Doug Flutie play than ever before—and he was simply magical. Scrambling, changing plays at the line of scrimmage, doing everything he could to engineer a stirring come-from-behind victory that made him the most talked-about college football player of the year.

He followed up that impressive performance with an even more spectacular exhibition of his skills when Boston played North Carolina. Doug completed every single one of his first 20 passes! He finished with 28 pass completions in 38 attempts. His total yardage gained through the air was 354! And he set a Boston College record of *six* touchdown passes. The most remarkable statistic of all, however, is that he did all of that in just over two quarters! Boston College was so far ahead early in the third quarter that Coach Bicknell took Doug out of the game. The final score was Boston 52, North Carolina 20. Bicknell called the North Carolina contest "probably Doug's best all-around game."

Doug went from great to terrible in one week, though, throwing three interceptions in his next game. Yet he was still the leader on the field and his scrambling and leadership helped the team pull out a 24-10 victory over Temple.

With a record of 4-0, Boston College was ranked #4 in the country. But their next opponent was their old nemesis, West Virginia. Doug played well, but not well enough to squeak out the victory. They lost a heartbreaker, 21-20, and fell to #11 in the national rankings. West Virginia was the only college team that Doug played against more than once without being able to engineer at least one victory.

Fighting back from that depressing loss, Doug threw for 318 yards and two touchdowns to defeat Rutgers, 35-23. Then came Penn State again. Doug threw for an astounding 447 yards, but it couldn't offset his two interceptions and Boston's three fumbles. In another close finish, Boston lost, 37-30. It was during this game, however, that Doug became the *first college player in history* to gain over 10,000 yards in total offense.

Boston College had a record of 5 wins and 2 losses. They couldn't afford to lose again if they were going to get a bowl invitation and if Doug was going to have his shot at the Heisman Trophy. The pressure was on. And Doug responded.

He led the Eagles past Army, 45-31, throwing for 311 yards and three touchdowns. Next, Doug and the Eagles took on Syracuse, and beat them 24-16.

Just before the famous Miami game that featured "The Pass," Boston College was invited to play in the Cotton Bowl. All they needed was a good showing against Miami to prove that they belonged in such an important bowl game.

They did more than just make a good showing. "The Pass" has become a legend in college football, and that game ranks as one of the most exciting of all time. B.C.'s incredible 47-45 victory was the standout moment of the entire season.

A lot of people have forgotten, though, that the Miami game wasn't the end of the regular season. Boston still had one more game to play before they faced Houston on New Year's Day. That game was against Holy Cross . . . and Boston crushed them 45-10. But it wasn't the score or the individual statistics of that game that mattered to Doug. It was in this game that Doug enjoyed one of his greatest thrills as a quarterback. He threw a touchdown pass to his kid brother, Darren!

Early in the fourth quarter, with Boston way ahead, Coach Bicknell took Doug out of the game. When it was over, his teammates—the guys he had led to a 9-2 season—lifted him up on their shoulders and carried him off the field. It was a grand moment as the whole team publicly showed their appreciation and their affection for Doug. It was a tribute that none of them would ever forget.

It was a day full of emotion. Only four hours after the end of the Holy Cross game, Doug was in New York with the other Heisman Trophy candidates, waiting to see if this time his name would be called.

It was.

His father cried with joy and pride.

In Doug's speech, he said, "When you're all alone, all by yourself, you wonder how it all happened."

The press went crazy. They couldn't get enough of him. He was on the cover of *Sports*

Illustrated (for the second time), he was interviewed constantly, he was asked to appear on *The Johnny Carson Show*—he was *the* topic of conversation for anyone who cared about football.

Then, almost as a break for Doug, it was time to get back to work and get ready for the Cotton Bowl. Coach Bicknell protected him from the press and they prepared for what would be Doug's last game as an Eagle.

It was rainy and miserable in Dallas on New Year's Day. But that didn't stop Doug from tying a Cotton Bowl record with three touchdown passes—and he reached that record while they were still in the second quarter!

Between the wind and rain, though, Doug started having problems. His receivers were slipping and falling, and the ball was hard to grip. He threw an interception that was run back for a Houston touchdown. The score was 31-28, with Boston hanging on for dear life.

While the defense was out on the field trying to keep Houston in check, Doug called a meeting of the offense. He told them, "Guys; I know we can move the ball. Let's go out and do it!"

The defense had done its job, and now the Eagles' offense came out on the field. They pounded out the yardage on the ground, scoring on a handoff from Doug to fullback Steve Strachan. And then they scored again on the ground. When the game was over, Boston had won a convincing 45-28 victory. And after two post-season defeats, Doug had finally brought a bowl game victory to Boston College.

8
DOUG FLUTIE . . . PRO!

Doug set college football records that may not be broken for a very long time. He finished his Boston College career with the highest passing yardage in history: 10,579 yards. He was also the all-time leader in total offense (passes and running yardage) with 11,054 yards. And, of course, he was the Heisman Trophy winner. Anybody else with those calling cards would be a shoo-in for pro football stardom. But at 5'9", Doug Flutie *still* hadn't convinced the skeptics.

Ray Perkins, the Alabama head coach who had previously coached the NFL's New York Giants, was quoted as saying, "I think he [Doug] would have a tough time in the NFL simply because the guys are a lot bigger in the NFL than they are in college. . . . Some people don't think height means that much, but I'll guarantee that it does."

Doug's response to that was simply, "That's his opinion and he's entitled to it."

All Doug wanted was a chance to show what he could do.

And there were a lot of people who wanted

to see Doug get his chance. There wasn't a single college senior who generated as much excitement on the field as Flutie, and that meant he was the kind of player who could sell tickets. The press was writing about him nearly every day. The question on every football fan's lips was who would get Doug Flutie—the NFL or the USFL?

In the NFL, the Buffalo Bills had the first pick in the college draft. It almost certainly would have to be Flutie. The fans in Buffalo were demanding it. But the Bills were strangely quiet despite the fact that the media kept Doug Flutie's name in front of the public. The Buffalo management couldn't seem to make up its mind if they wanted to make Doug an offer or trade their first-round draft choice to another team.

At first, Doug publicly stated that he had no preference between the NFL and USFL. He'd make his decision based on the best offer. But it seemed at the beginning that if the two offers were roughly alike, Doug would opt to play in the NFL. He is enormously competitive and there's no question that at this point, the NFL is seen by most people as a tougher league. Doug would have wanted to prove himself. He'd want to show the skeptics—once and for all—what kind of football player he really was.

But Doug wasn't getting that chance. The

Buffalo Bills refused to get serious about negotiating. It seemed as if they were hoping that all the media hoopla about Doug would die down so that they wouldn't have to pay him as much money as the press seemed to think he was worth. They were playing a waiting game.

Except Doug didn't want to wait. And neither did Donald Trump, owner of the New Jersey Generals.

Donald Trump wasn't about to wait for the Bills or any other NFL team to finally make their move. Doug Flutie was a major celebrity all over the country. He was handsome, well-spoken, and every inch a star. Flutie was just what Mr. Trump needed to grab attention for his team and his league.

Trump said, "Flutie represents a young dynamic force." And he wanted that "young dynamic force" on his team. Before the NFL could react, Donald Trump offered Doug a package worth roughly $8,000,000 to sign with the New Jersey Generals. Trump was doing the same thing the New York Jets had done when they signed Joe Namath for what was then an astronomical $400,000. Namath gave instant credibility the old American Football League —instant credibility and big box office appeal.

The big question was, would Doug Flutie sign the contract? There were those who thought that Flutie was using Trump's offer to force the Buffalo Bills into negotiating. Trump wasn't about to let that happen. He publicly announced that the offer to Doug Flutie was based on the interest in him NOW. The longer Doug waited, the less he'd be worth to the Generals.

Doug was on the spot. He'd be losing money every day he waited for Buffalo to make an offer. And it was in Buffalo's favor now to wait as long as possible so that they wouldn't be competing with Mr. Trump's millions.

Doug was playing for the highest stakes he had ever played for in his life—because it *was* his life.

It was like fourth and goal to go on the one-yard line. Should you go for the sure three points or risk it all by going for the touchdown? The only difference was that Doug knew that this was not a game. He had just this one decision to make and it would affect the rest of his life forever. He did what any smart play-caller would do—he took the sure thing.

There were probably a lot of reasons why Doug signed with the Generals. Besides the very substantial appeal of the money, one of the key factors was that he'd be playing in the media capital of the world. The Big Apple. Being a star in New York is worth a fortune in television commercials and personal appearances. Playing in New York means fame. Giants

Stadium, where the Generals play their home games, is actually in New Jersey, but it is only a few minutes from New York City.

While Doug would surely have liked to test himself in the NFL, he must have also realized that the career of a pro football player can be over in the time it takes a linebacker to bend your knee in the wrong direction. In other words, you can have a very short life as a pro. With his plans to marry and have a family, Doug clearly wanted to know that if anything happened to him, his future wife and children would always be cared for. And who knows, maybe the USFL will ultimately merge with the NFL. If that should happen, Doug will be the biggest winner of all.

Doug's decision to play for the New Jersey Generals meant that he had to play two football seasons back-to-back. He'd finish his college courses and get his degree later, because he had to begin immediately preparing for the USFL's spring schedule.

The Generals traded away Brian Sipe, their experienced quarterback who had had a long, successful career with the Cleveland Browns in the NFL. It was all on Doug's shoulders now, and he had precious little time to get ready. Everything was new. He had to learn a whole new system, new coaches, new players. Thrust into this difficult situation, no one should have expected him to be an instant hero. But they did.

The Generals got off to a rocky start, losing their opening game against Birmingham, 38-28. Doug admitted to being nervous and a little tight. Because of it, he tended to overthrow his receivers. Doug played a little better in the next game, and the Generals defeated Orlando.

The Los Angeles Express, with Steve Young at quarterback, came to the Meadowlands to play the Generals in New Jersey's home opener. A huge crowd of more than 58,000 fans came out to see Doug Flutie's hometown debut. And they weren't sorry they did. Between Herschel Walker's running and Doug Flutie's scrambling and passing, the Generals beat Los Angeles 35-24.

Then everything fell apart during the next game. They lost at Baltimore 29-9 and looked bad. They held on in their next game to defeat Tampa Bay, 28-24. But then they were murdered again, 31-13, by Arizona.

With a mediocre 3-3 record, some people were starting to question whether Flutie could really do the job. But Doug knew that he could. He just needed a little bit more time to prove it. And in the next four games, he and Herschel Walker showed what two Heisman Trophy winners could do! They reeled off four straight victories, beating Houston 31-25, Portland 34-7, Memphis 21-18, and again Orlando 24-7.

After the Orlando game, Doug was asked if he had tried to do too much when he first came to the Generals. "I think a lot was expected of me," he replied. "Originally, the idea was to run Herschel and keep the heat off me, and try to get it going that way—the way we're doing it right now. But we weren't running the ball well early in the season. It just took a while to come together as a team. We all wanted to do well. I wanted to do well, the guys on the team wanted me to do well. We weren't rushing things, but we were pressing a little bit. I wanted to step in the first day and take over— that's the way I am. But it was going to take time. The coaching staff, obviously, did an excellent job of handling the situation, because we came back."

Doug was obviously pleased with the way the team was shaping up late in the season. "It's a great atmosphere here," he said. "When someone makes a big play, everyone's patting him on the back—whether it's an offensive player, a defensive player, or a field-goal kicker. We're really a together group, and I don't think we were there early in the season. I think it's come with the length of the season, and as the season goes on, we're coming closer and closer together, which is the key factor for the team."

But, he said, "You can always get better. You can always throw one more completion; you can always score one more touchdown; you can always have one less penalty. There's always room for improvement."

Two of Orlando's quarterbacks were knocked out of the game with injuries during their second game against the Generals. Doug was asked what he thought about that—especially since he was the one everyone was afraid would get hurt because of his size. It's a difficult subject for him to talk about. "I always wince a little bit when I see quarterbacks go down," he said. "I know that can be me someday, so I just sort of hold my breath. It's a matter of luck and a matter of coincidence sometimes, and you just have to be thankful for it and just hope it keeps up." Is that why he runs so fast? He laughed. "That's why I *try* to run fast."

But Doug doesn't always take the safest route when he's scrambling for a gainer. While most of the time he'll safely scamper out of bounds or slide to the ground just before he's about to be tackled, Doug explained that, "You can be careful every now and then to avoid unnecessary hits, but you can't play cautious." It scares his coaches, but he's too competitive not to run for big yardage if he thinks he can make it.

His attitude matches the USFL's—at least in the area of not being cautious. With the league voting to play in the fall in 1986, the Generals will be competing against the Jets and the Giants for fans. That's fine with Doug.

"I'm real excited about the move to the fall," he said. "It'll give me some time to buy a house—get settled in. Also, we'll be playing football in the *fall*—which is what I'm used to, what everyone is accustomed to doing. The one thing that bums me out," he added, "is that I won't be able to see all the B.C. games."

Doug doesn't worry about the Generals losing fans to the Jets and Giants. "We're gonna have our share of the fans. Maybe they'll think we're more exciting than the Jets and the Giants and they'll want to come see us." For those who've seen Doug Flutie in action, they already know that exciting football is the only kind of football he knows how to play!

Doug captured the hearts of his hometown fans in Natick, Massachusetts, when he played for his high school team; he captured the hearts of all of New England when he brought glory to Boston College; and he captured the hearts of football fans everywhere when "the kid" showed he could do it as a pro. It's no wonder then that whenever Doug makes a great play, the fans start chanting: *"FLOOOOTIE . . . FLOOOOTIE . . . FLOOOTIE!"*

9
The Future Is Now!

On June 1, 1985, during the first half of the Memphis game, Doug scrambled forward on a running play. He was over the line of scrimmage and just about to break it open for good yardage when he was tackled by the 305-pound Reggie White.

Doug didn't get up . . . his collarbone was broken.

It was the end of his season. He never played another down (although he was suited up for the playoff game against the Baltimore Stars). It was a big disappointment for Doug and his fans, but the excitement he generated throughout the season suggests that this year was only the beginning of what will be a legendary career.

Though Doug's first-year pro statistics don't appear to be all that outstanding, the ultimate statistic that all quarterbacks are judged by is did their team win or lose. And by that standard, Doug was indeed a winner. At the time he was injured, Doug had brought the Generals to an impressive 10-5 won/lost record.

To put it another way, you don't win games with statistics, you win them by leading your team down the field and across the goal line. And Doug has always had an uncanny knack for doing just that. It is also often forgotten that this twenty-two-year-old athlete has played under possibly the most pressure-filled circumstances of anyone in sports history.

Think of it: He began the year in training camp in August of 1984 to prepare for his last season as a college player. Then, during his record-breaking year at Boston College, he was constantly besieged by reporters and cameras. After "The Pass," the Cotton Bowl victory, and the Heisman Trophy, Doug was understandably exhausted. But there was no time to rest. (It was now January of 1985.) He played more post-season college football, signed his ballyhooed contract with the Generals, and had to step in and lead the team with almost no practice time. Remember, it normally takes three years to learn the quarterback position in the pros. Doug barely had three weeks!

Playing in the New York City area, which is media capital of the world, every incompletion and interception was magnified by TV and newspaper reporters. So much was expected of Doug that on several occasions in Giants Stadium he was booed after a bad set of downs.

And that despite the fact that, at that time, Doug had not lost a single game at home!

Doug himself has talked about the attention paid to his statistics and he's been quite honest. "You'd like to put up some flashy stats," he admitted to a reporter. "Obviously if you had them you'd be helping your team." But Doug pointed out that those who *only* point at statistics have "their priorities out of whack. I'm shooting for the sky, for the championship, and I'm still on the road to my goal," he said.

He didn't get his championship this year, the injury took care of that, but you can bet he'll win one someday . . . and probably very soon.

While this has been a difficult season for Doug, it's also been a year of tremendous growth. Doug's only interest in the past was sports, but he's come to appreciate that there is more to life than winning football games.

He's become very good friends with his teammate and fellow Heisman Trophy winner, Herschel Walker. "It's nice to have a Herschel Walker in your backfield," Doug said recently, "but what's nicer is being able to talk to Herschel off the field. He gave me a chance to have a friend. We very rarely talk about football, about what the press is saying, about people's expectations, the game this week. That's helped me to keep things in perspective."

And keeping himself in perspective means seeing himself as somethng more than a football player. This young man who has already given football fans a full career's worth of thrills has made a point of sharing the limelight with others. In an admirable show of generosity, he insisted that when he was to be filmed in a TV commercial for Ford trucks,that his old college friend Gerard Phelan, the teammate who had been on the receiving end of THE PASS, had to be included (and paid!). When Doug did a Hamilton Beach commercial, he insisted that his New Jersey Generals teammates also be on screen (and paid!).

But these are the public things that Doug has done. Far less known are his private gestures. It's only by accident that it was learned that Doug went to a dance held at Cedar Grove Memorial High School in New Jersey to benefit a girl who had become blind from diabetes. The girl's name is Leanne, but Doug didn't know her. He had heard about the dance and that she was a fan of his. So, unannounced, with no press people around to turn his appearance into a media circus, Doug arrived and danced with Leanne.

He never told anyone in the press or anyone with the Generals about it. It came out only after a boy in Leanne's high school class wrote Doug a letter of thanks. Unknown to Doug, the letter was passed to a reporter.

Who knows what other kind gestures Doug has made that have never reached the press? But if Doug has his way, they never will. That's the way Doug is . . . and that's one of the reasons he's so special.

Both on and off the field, Doug Flutie has shown himself to be a winner in every way. Though his first year as a pro wasn't all he had hoped it would be, it was far better than anyone could have realistically expected. And that speaks well for the years ahead. The championship ring he wants so badly is sure to finally catch up to him. With his talent and unique style, you can bet that Doug Flutie is first-and-goal-to-go on the drive to greatness!

STATISTICS

College Records:

- Most yards gained in total offense in a career: 11,317
- Most yards gained in passing yardage in a career: 10,579
- Most yards per pass completion in a career (minimum 400 completions): 15.6
- Most total yards gained against on opponent in a career: 1,445 vs. Penn State, 1981-84.
- Most yards gained by two players in one game: 953 (the famous Miami game—Flutie with 517, Bernie Kosar with 436)

College Awards:

1984—
- Heisman Trophy Winner
- Player of the Year, *UPI*
- Player of the Year, *The Sporting News*
- First-Team All America, *AP, UPI*
- Rhodes Scholarship Nominee

1983—
- Third place, Heisman Trophy
- Liberty Bowl Most Valuable Player
- All America—Second Team, *UPI*

1982—
- Tangerine Bowl Most Outstanding Offensive Player

1981—
- ECAC Co-Rookie of the Year

College Statistics:

Completions	Percentage	Yards	Int.	TD	W/L
1984—					
233-386	.604	3,454	11	27	9-2
1983—					
194-381	.509	3,011	16	20	9-2
1982—					
184-386	.477	3,048	22	15	7-2-1
1981—					
105-192	.547	1,652	8	10	5-4*

*Includes Penn State game entered in 4th quarter.

Pro Statistics:

1985 Passing—

Attempts	Comp.	Yards	Int.	TD	W/L
280	134	2,109	13	13	10-5

1985 Rushing—

Carries	Yards	TD
67	460	6

**Other Books in the
Avon Superstar Series:**

Marino/Montana—$2.50

An action packed biography of the two best quarterbacks in the N.F.L., Dan Marino of the Miami Dolphins and Joe Montana of the San Francisco Forty Niners who faced each other in Superbowl XIX.

Includes 16 pages of black and white photographs!

More to come! Ask for them in your bookstore.

Paperback